Quilled
Birds, Bugs & Butterflies

EM
Elizabeth Moad

www.elizabethmoad.com

First Published in 2011

ISBN 978-0-9566209-1-0

Printed in the UK by The Lavenham Press Ltd
Editor: Jo Richardson
Designers: Sarah Wade and Peter Evans Uk Ltd
Photographer: Karl Adamson

www.elizabethmoad.com

CONTENTS

INTRODUCTION

The idea for this book came from my realization that, throughout a decade of quilling, there are certain themes that recur time and time again. Butterflies, for example, are often the very first quilled motif beginners make, as they are easy to create in their basic form, but they continue to feature because they are a much-loved image. Birds of all kinds and proportions have also followed me down the quilling years, and I have had great fun developing them in quilling form, from the traditional to the fabulous. And bugs have also become a firm favourite not least because of their versatility – they can be cute or scary and appropriate for children's cards or those for gardeners or nature lovers. So it has been a great pleasure for me to consolidate all three popular themes in one book to share with other followers of the thrilling craft of quilling.

Throughout this sourcebook of ideas, the quilled motifs decorate cards and tags in a mix of shapes and sizes for you to create striking designs for different purposes and individuals. For any crafter, giving a handmade card as opposed to a mass-produced shop-bought one is an essential part of everyday life. The recipient will never fail to recognize the thought and care that has been put into creating a handcrafted card and will always appreciate it. And any quilled card will stand out an especially long way from commercial designs. Even beginners in the craft I have known have hesitantly sent their first attempts to family and friends to then receive such positive feedback that it has boosted their confidence and spurred them on.

The intricacies of quilling offer a variety of intriguing effects, and in this book I have assembled a range of quilling card projects exploring that wonderful diversity for you to dip into. Each design is presented with a step-by-step guide to the particular techniques involved, to ensure successful results. Here, quilling is used to make traditional motifs such as a Partridge in a Pear Tree (see pages 38–39), but it is also given a modern twist using vibrant tones and bold compositions to bring it bang up to date, with inspiration drawn from the contemporary colour schemes and cutting-edge design ideas that crop up each year. Although there is a wealth of ideas for you to choose from, don't be afraid to adapt a design to suit your personal colour preferences or those of the recipient.

A POTTED HISTORY OF QUILLING

Paper quilling, or paper filigree as it is sometimes called, has its roots in history around 500 years ago. The exact origins are not known, as paper degrades over time, but it is thought that the first quillers were among members of religious households who created paper art for devotional purposes. Examples dating back to Georgian and Victorian times do still exist, when decorating tea caddies and boxes with rolled paper shapes was regarded as an appropriate leisure pursuit for ladies. The papers were rolled around the quills of bird feathers, and this was how the craft gained its name. Quilling became popular in England in the late 18th and early 19th centuries and from here it spread to the American colonies. Quilling subsequently suffered a decline, but it has since resurfaced to become a popular 21st-century craft that is practised throughout the world.

QUILLING IN DAY-TO-DAY LIFE

For many of us, quilling has to fit in with our daily lives and can only be slotted in once all our chores are done or after a day at work. Some crafters are able to take over a spare room (once the children have left home!) and can enjoy the luxury of a dedicated area where they can sit down and get quilling. But many others have just a corner of a room available and a limited amount of space. Fortunately, quilling is a craft that doesn't need much in the way of equipment, just a few papers, small tools and glue – the essentials fit into a shoebox. Nevertheless, you will find yourself building up tools and gadgets over time, so some organization and means of storage is eventually needed.

The advice I give to beginners is not to be too ambitious in trying to tackle a large project in the first instance but rather to start with a quick and easy one such as Butterfly Bunch, pages 18–19. Once you have gained confidence in coiling and pinching, you can move on to a more complex project such as Singing Bluebirds, pages 30–31, and in no time at all every kind of bird, bug and butterfly in the book will be appearing on your work desk!

PRACTICAL TIPS

- Always work in good light with a desk lamp so that you don't strain your eyes.

- Gluing is a critical part of quilling, and if the glue is the wrong sort, the papers will not stick properly (see page 8 for glue).

- Buy ready-cut paper strips from established quilling suppliers so that the weight of paper is correct (see page 6 for papers and storage).

- Wash your hands before quilling to remove grease and grime, and cool hands are better than sweaty ones!

- Check that the quilled design is glued on securely so that the coils don't fall off in the post.

- Take extra care when adding a greeting or message to cards – this is often the final part to be completed and a design can be ruined if it's rushed.

- Make matching tags for gifts by taking an element from the main card design.

- Plan postage and buy ready-made posting boxes so that your quilling doesn't arrive crushed.

- Enjoy your quilling and the results will show – if you are having a bad day and your quilling is going wrong, take a break and come back to it refreshed!

PAPERS

As eggs are to an omelette, paper is the one single, key ingredient for quilling, and the foundation of the whole technique. It's possible to cut your own strips of paper, but most quillers purchase pre-cut strips to the width they require in the colours they want. Pre-cut strips not only save time but they are exactly uniform in width. Many suppliers will trim paper to the width you require, but wider strips will tend to cost slightly more. Quilling is not an expensive hobby, so do indulge in some extra-special papers for your cards.

COLOUR

Nature allows you to use any colour, so don't be restricted to dull shades but instead explore bright pinks, reds and combinations of harmonious tones. Metallic-edged papers are very popular, as they shimmer and glint in the light – ideal for quilled shapes.

WEIGHTS

The weight of paper used for quilling is critical and this is why it's best to purchase strips rather than cut your own. The paper should be around 100gsm in weight, which is strong enough to coil easily and hold it shape. Paper of a lighter weight isn't easy to work with because it's too flimsy, and conversely paper that's relatively heavy or thick is too stiff to coil.

WIDTHS

Pre-cut paper strips come in several standard widths, as personal preference varies with the crafter, and the choice of width will also depend on what is being made. The following widths of paper are used this book:

1.5–2mm (1/16in) – the minimum width that's available
3mm (1/8in) – this is the most common width and ideal for beginners
5mm (3/16in) – this width is good for more definition
10mm (3/8in) – this is the most common width for use with a fringing tool

STORAGE

If you are a beginner to quilling, once you have accumulated your quilling papers it's important to store them so that they are easily accessible and won't become tangled. Plastic storage units are readily available and inexpensive, allowing you to organize the papers according to colour, width and special finishes.

QUILLING TOOLS

I have always used a quilling tool – the one pictured here – and teach classes using a tool because I find it easy to use and to achieve quick results. A quilling tool has a two-pronged slot through which to thread paper, and the handle makes it easy to turn for coiling. However, not all quillers use a tool to make coils, as some prefer to make them by rolling the paper around a needle tool or just using their fingers. The advantage of a quilling tool is that the slot catches the end of the paper, whereas the needle tool requires the paper to be wrapped around it. The disadvantage of the quilling tool is that it leaves a kink in the centre of the coil, which coiling around a needle tool does not. There are times when I don't want this kink, and in those cases I use a needle tool or a needle in a cork, so a combination of both methods is a practical approach. But it is of course a matter of personal preference and I never prescribe what to use – as long as people are quilling, I'm happy!

My quilling tool is used throughout this book, as pictured left and above from Partridge in a Pear Tree, pages 38–39. It has travelled far and wide with me across the world, and miraculously I haven't managed to lose it!

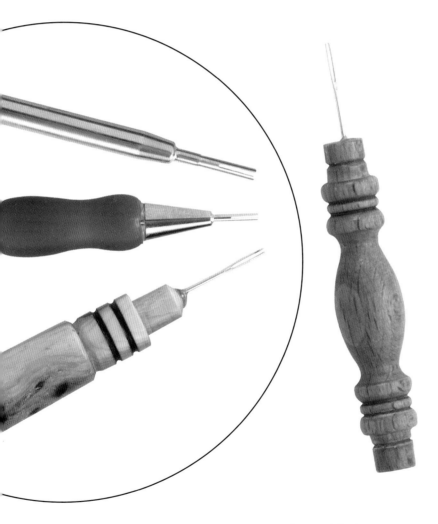

The wooden quilling tools shown here are sewing needles with one end snipped off, embedded into a wooden handle. These have a narrow gap, just wide enough to slot the paper through, thus creating a very small centre in a tight coil.

Quilling tools come in all shapes and sizes, but are all essentially the same design with a slot for the paper and a handle. Quilling tools can be very cheap to purchase, but even the most expensive is not a lot of money and they last a lifetime with care. I have used the same tool for 10 years. It is, however, important to find the tool that suits you. Some people prefer long handles, while others favour shorter handles that fit into the palm of the hand. When choosing a quilling tool, look at the size of the gap at the curling end: a larger gap in the tool means a large gap in the centre of the coil and this is most noticeable when making tight coils.

QUILLING KIT

The following is a guide to the basic essentials needed for quilling. This is not an exhaustive list and more experienced crafters may use other tools and embellishing materials.

BASIC TOOLS

Cutting mat, craft knife and metal ruler

A self-healing cutting mat is essential when cutting with a craft knife and metal ruler, and also protects your work surface.

Fine-tipped tweezers

These are used for picking up, pinching and positioning coils, gemstones and so on. The pair shown is self-locking so that you don't need to keep them squeezed.

PVA (white) glue

It's best to use a tacky PVA (white) glue, as it dries quickly and is not too runny. Apply the glue with a cocktail stick (toothpick).

Large circle punch or shape cutter and template

You should use one or other of these tools for cutting large circles from card, such as a circle aperture in a card blank, to achieve a professional finish.

Needle tool

This is a metal point on a handle, useful for rolling paper around and leaving a hole in the centre. Some quillers like to use a needle tool for applying a dot of glue instead of a cocktail stick (toothpick).

Small, fine-pointed scissors

Essential for snipping and trimming papers.

HB pencil and eraser

Required for marking lines on graph paper and for tracing templates.

Quilling board

This template board is cork- or foam-based with a plastic top that has cut-out circles of various sizes. The cork or foam is recessed, allowing you to insert a coil and let it unwind while constrained by the plastic edges. A quilling board allows you to create exactly the same size of coil every time.

Fringing tool

These tools are so called because they 'fringe' paper. By manually moving the handle of the tool up and down, the paper is sliced at a 90-degree angle. However, it doesn't cut right across the paper but leaves an uncut margin so that the paper stays in one piece. As you move the handle up and down, the paper is pulled through so that you can fringe a whole length in no time at all.

Board and pins

Used for the husking technique (see pages 50–51), a thick piece of foam, polystyrene or Styrofoam board allows pins to be inserted in order to position and hold papers in place.

EMBELLISHING TOOLS AND MATERIALS

Quilled designs can be decorated or enhanced with a few extra items, and here is a representative selection of the additional tools and materials used in the book.

Glitter glue

Easier to apply than traditional dry glitter, this glue allows more precise application using the nozzle.

Small circle punches

Use a small circle punch to make a clean hole in a tag, through which to thread ribbon (see Fab Flamingo Tag, page 24, Translucent Butterfly Tag, page 27, and Bee Well, page 33).

Pattern-edged scissors

Used to cut card, such as in Singing Bluebirds, pages 30–31, and Fabulously Framed, page 44, these scissors are a useful toolbox addition.

Shimmer paint

This specialist metallic paint comes in small pots and is mixed with water and painted on to add a vibrant finish. It's easy to use, as you can see in Dainty Dragonflies, pages 40–41, and can be applied to many other quilling projects.

Wiggly eyes

These are eyes that move around and are great for bringing quilled birds, bugs and butterflies to life, such as the Ladybird Cuties on pages 36–37.

Basic Techniques

In quilling, the end result is determined by the length of paper used, how much the coil is allowed to unwind and if the end of the coiled paper is glued in place. These three factors are explored and demonstrated here.

How to Make a Coil

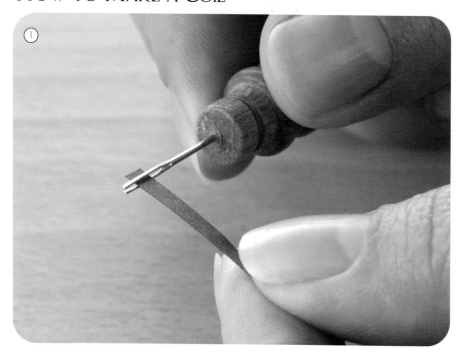

1 Insert a strip of paper into the slot of the quilling tool 2mm (1/16in) from the end of the paper. If you are a beginner, it's best to use 3mm (1/8in) wide paper, which is the width used in these examples.

2 Turn the quilling tool to catch the end of the paper strip. Continue to turn the tool. I always turn the tool away from me, as I find this gives me most control, but there is no hard and fast rule. Guide the coil with your fingers and keep a light tension on the paper with your spare hand.

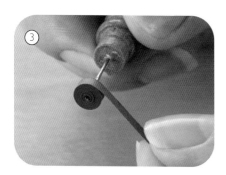

3 Continue turning the quilling tool until the end of the paper is reached, then carefully remove the tool by sliding the paper off the prongs, holding the coiled paper in place.

4 Release the coil a little and then glue the end of the strip to the coil to create a loose closed coil.

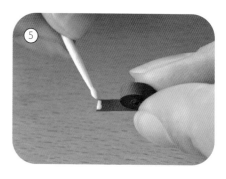

5 Alternatively, without releasing the coil, add a dot of glue to the end of the strip with a cocktail stick (toothpick) and press to the coil to make a tight coil.

6 If you release the coil further, the coil will become larger in diameter.

7 Release the coil even further or let go altogether to create an open coil.

8 Apply a small amount of PVA (white) glue over one side of the coil, making sure that the centre and outer edges have glue on.

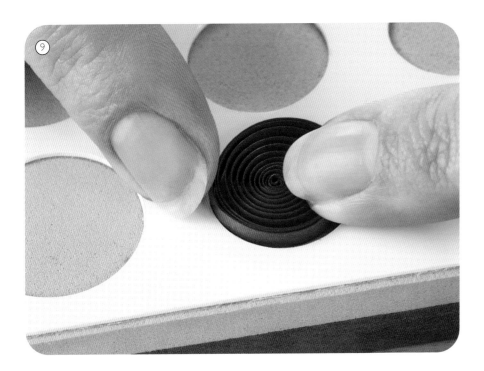

9 Alternatively, insert the coil into a template in a quilling board to achieve a specific size of coil. A quilling board is used in Spiralling Butterflies, pages 26–27, to make the coils for the wings identical.

Loose Closed Coils

These are shapes that are created where the end of the paper has been glued to the coil. Here, the initial coil has been allowed to unwind a little and become loose, but the coil is closed.

Teardrop Pinch one end to a point.

Bent teardrop Pinch one end and then pull this point round at an angle.

Off-centre teardrop Pull the centre of the coil to one side and make sure that the inner coils are evenly spaced, then pinch on that side.

Eye (sometimes called a marquise) Pinch at two opposing points.

Triangle Pinch at three points an equal distance apart.

Square Pinch at two points as for the eye and then pinch at another equally spaced two points.

Diamond Pinch as for the square, but squeeze gently at two points.

Crescent Pinch at two opposing points, then pull the pinched points round and inwards to bend.

This Guardian Owl (see page 49) demonstrates the use of different pinched shapes, such as the crescent and diamond.

Loose Closed Coils

Rectangle Pinch at two opposing points, then pinch again at two opposing points a short distance from the first two pinched points.

Star Pinch at four equally spaced points and then press inwards towards the centre.

Half circle Pinch at two points relatively close together, leaving the curve of the coil intact on the opposite side of the coil.

Heart Pinch into a teardrop, hold the point in one hand and simultaneously push inwards with a fingernail at the opposing point.

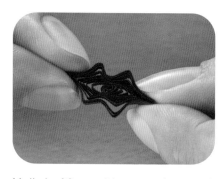

Holly leaf Start with an eye shape and then holding the centre with tweezers, push the outer points inwards.

This Sedate Swan card (see page 42) is an example of how the coiled shapes can be manipulated to create a striking, expressive image.

Open Coils

For open coils, the paper is coiled with the quilling tool, then the tool removed and the coil left to find its own shape without being glued at all. As the end of the paper is not glued and is left 'open', this is why they are known as open coils.

The variety of these open coils is endless because the length of paper can be folded at differing points and the ends coiled. Open coils are generally used in conjunction with pinched loose closed coils and other quilling techniques such as huskings to add variation to the designs, for example in Love Bugs, page 23, Spiralling Butterflies, pages 26–27, and Bejewelled Butterfly, pages 50–51.

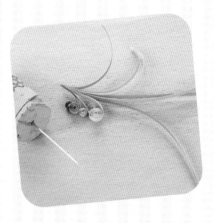

A needle tool is used to roll paper around to create the open coils in Fancy Birds, pages 20–21, the preferred tool in this instance to avoid the kink that a quilling tool leaves.

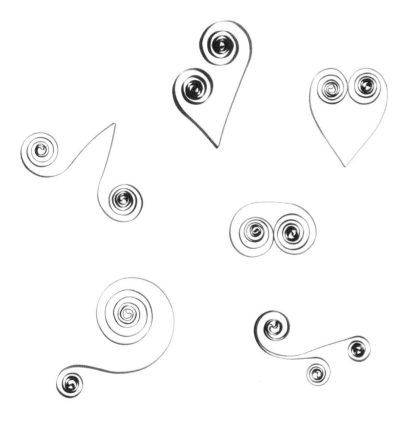

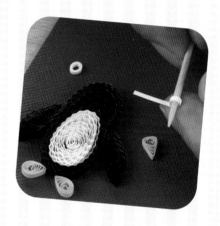

Other tools can be used to make open coils and quilled shapes. Here, paper is wound around a cocktail stick (toothpick) in Friendly Penguins, pages 46–47, to make a closed coil with a large open centre. A cocktail stick (toothpick) could also be used in place of a needle tool.

Open coils are used to create the flamboyant swirly tail feathers of the Fancy Birds on pages 20–21, including these Love Birds. Using several lengths of paper in this way adds a light flourish to the more solid quilled shapes.

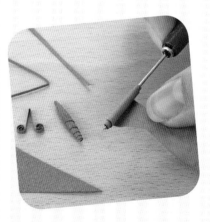

If you don't have a needle tool, make your own by setting a fine sewing needle into a dense wine cork.

PROJECTS

Happy Birthday

Happy Christmas

10

Happy Birthday

Butterfly *bunch*

There are an infinite number of ways to quill a butterfly, but we are often short of time and need a fast version. Here, a single basic form of butterfly is made in different colours to create a pretty flock that flutter around dainty pale green flower sprigs. The butterfly wings are pinched loose closed coils glued at an angle to a folded body to give dimension, while the flower sprigs are made from pinched coils glued either side of a main stem. Two different sizes of butterfly are created simply by changing the size of the coils. These butterfly cards can be used for most occasions from birthday to sympathy.

You will need…

- papers: 3mm (1/8in) brown, red, pale green, pink, purple, turquoise, mauve; 1.5mm (1/16in) brown
- turquoise card
- eraser wedges or similar
- purple card blank

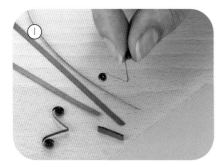

1 To make a butterfly body, fold over a 10cm (4in) length of brown 3mm (1/8in) paper at 1cm (3/8in) intervals and glue at each fold until the end is reached. For the antennae, fold a 10cm (4in) length of 1.5mm (1/16in) brown paper in half, then coil either end to the centre. Pinch the coils flat. Glue the body and antennae to a square of turquoise card.

2 To make the wings for a red butterfly, take a 40cm (153/4in) length of 3mm (1/8in) red paper and make a loose closed coil. Pinch either end of the coil to make an eye shape (see page 12). Repeat for the second wing. Glue the first wing to the side of the body and prop up with a wedge – here, I have cut wedges from an eraser with a craft knife. Glue the other wing in place and prop up as before. Leave to dry, then remove the wedges.

3 For the flower heads, use 10cm (4in) lengths of 3mm (1/8in) pale green paper to make loose closed coils, then pinch into crescent shapes (see page 13). Glue a crescent shape to the turquoise card and place a dot of glue on the rounded edge. For the flower stem, press a strip of pale green paper onto the glue and glue another crescent to the other side of the stem. Continue gluing the crescents either side up the stem, using the photo opposite as a guide to positioning.

Sentiment Suggestions

Sending you warmest wishes
For a special friend
With deepest sympathy
Missing you

Hanging Delights

For this lively design, a circle is cut in a purple card blank and then a smaller circle of green card suspended in the aperture. This is achieved by tying a length of pale purple organza ribbon around the centre of the card blank front, finishing in a pretty bow at the top, then backing the green card circle with another so that the ribbon is sandwiched between. A single flower sprig decorates the central circle together with three butterflies of different colours. Two smaller butterflies are then attached bottom left and top right of the card blank.

Tip ...

Glitter could be added to
the wings as in Spiralling
Butterflies, pages 26–27,
or gemstones, as in
Bejewelled Butterfly,
pages 50–51.

Finishing the card

Continue to make flower sprigs and glue to the bottom left-hand corner of
the turquoise card as shown above. To add variation, join two stems together
near the base. Make another red butterfly, then one pink, one purple and one
turquoise. For the smaller mauve butterflies, make the bodies and antennae in
the same dimensions as before but then form the wings from 20cm (8in)
lengths. Position one of these butterflies to nestle among the flowers. Mount
the turquoise card onto a slightly larger purple card blank.

Butterfly Trio

An elegant portrait-shaped version of the main card is created here featuring
a tall sprig of flowers trailing up the left-hand side of the card with three
large butterflies fluttering up the right-hand side, two turquoise and one red.
The calm, balanced feel of this design makes it ideal for a get well card or
sympathy and a message could be added directly onto the turquoise card in
the centre. For a short cut, the flower sprig could be rubber stamped instead
of quilled and then just the three butterflies attached.

Fancy *birds*

Quilling allows a lot of artistic licence, as you can see here in these fanciful birds with their showy twirled tails where the coils have taken over! The colour scheme of shades of blue and green creates a contemporary, fresh look. The wiggly eyes add an element of movement, while the spindly legs provide a comic contrast in proportion. The birds are made with 2mm (1/16in) papers for a finer finish but they could be made with 3mm (1/8in) strips instead. With their fun, modern feel, these cards would be perfect for teenage girls.

You will need ...

- papers: 2mm (1/16in) shades of blue and green, black; 3mm (1/8in) dark green, dark brown
- cream card
- 2 small wiggly eyes
- turquoise card blank

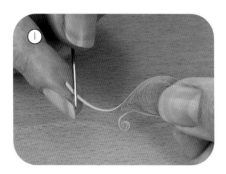

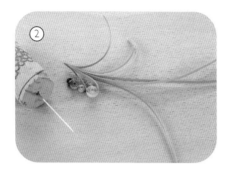

1 For the bird body, coil an 80cm (32in) length of 2mm (1/16in) blue paper and pinch one end. Take a 15cm (6in) length of 2mm (1/16in) green paper and wrap this around the edge of the blue coil just made, then glue in place around the edge but leave the two ends free as shown. Use a needle tool to coil the ends of the green paper outwards.

2 For the tail, glue three 5cm (2in) lengths of 2mm (1/16in) blue paper, then five to seven 10cm (4in) lengths of varying shades of 2mm (1/16in) blue and green and finally three 5cm (2in) lengths of blues and greens together at one end. Use a needle tool to make an open coil at the end of each length, coiling down to the glued end. Insert the glued end into the bird body left open in step 1. Make a second body and tail in the same way.

3 To make the spindly legs, fold 3cm (1 1/4in) lengths of 2mm (1/16in) black paper in half, concertina and then glue along the length. For the leaves, use 40cm (15 3/4in), 30cm (12in) and 20cm (8in) lengths of 3mm (1/8in) dark green paper to make loose closed coils, then pinch either end of the coils to make eye shapes (see page 12). For the main vertical branch, take an 80cm (32in) length of 3mm (1/8in) dark brown paper and make a small loop, then continue to loop, gradually increasing the size of the loops, until the end of the paper is reached.

Tip ...

These birds would look equally fantastic in other colour schemes such as pinks or purples.

Exotic Bird Tag

A fancy bird in flight makes a stunning, ideally shaped motif for a gift tag. The bird is made as for the main card to the same dimensions. The wing is wrapped with green paper to make it stand out. As this bird is flying there is no need to add legs. If the bird was made all in white and set against a soft-coloured background, it would make a wonderful wedding design.

Tip ...

A leaf rubber stamp could be used to make a background instead of quilled leaves, to save time and also to accentuate the quilling (see Ladybird Cuties, pages 36–37).

Finishing the card

Glue the main vertical branch onto a rectangle of cream card. Make two smaller looped branches each from a 40cm (153/4in) length of dark brown paper and attach horizontally. Glue the leaves in place around the branches. Attach the bird bodies with their tails and then the legs. Using tweezers and extra-strong glue, attach a small wiggly eye to each bird. Make a wing for each bird by coiling a 20cm (8in) length of 2mm (1/16in) blue or green paper into a loose closed coil and pinching into a teardrop shape (see page 12). Finally, for each head plume glue together one 5cm (2in) and two 3cm (11/4in) lengths of 2mm (1/16in) blue and green papers, then coil the ends outwards.

Love Birds

Here, two fancy birds, one blue and one green, meet beak to beak on branches with love in the air. The card has the fold at the top and is tied with organza ribbon. The branches are made by looping dark brown paper, as in the main card, with just a few leaves added to keep the overall design uncluttered. In this design, the birds are without wings and head plumes to keep it simpler. The quilled heart is formed from two teardrop shapes, each made with 20cm (8in) lengths of paper, glued together.

Ant army

This army of ants working hard to spell out 'Happy Birthday' is sure to raise a smile as well as being fun to make! The ants consist of three coils for the body with strips of paper sandwiched between for the legs. The paper strips are then creased to give the legs shape and movement. Wiggly eyes add character to these little bugs to make them extra appealing. The lettering is also quilled, using bright red paper so that it really stands out.

You will need ...

- papers: 3mm (1/8in) black, red; 2mm (1/16in) black
- 16 small wiggly eyes
- card: green, pale green
- dark green card blank

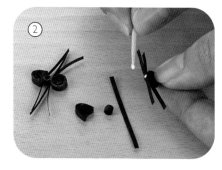

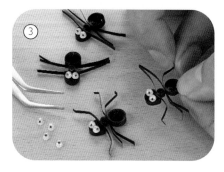

1 Each ant body is made from three loose closed coils. For the large body coil, use a 20cm (8in) length of 3mm (1/8in) black paper; for the middle smaller body coil a 5cm (2in) length and for the head a 15cm (6in) length. Pinch the head coils into a crescent shape (see page 13). It helps to set up a mini production line to make the three body parts.

2 For the ant legs, use 3.5cm (13/8in) lengths of 2mm (1/16in) black paper. Firstly, glue one length to the flat part of the crescent head shape, then glue the middle body coil to this. Glue two more 3.5cm (13/8in) lengths to the middle coil and finally attach the large body coil.

3 Using tweezers and extra-strong glue, attach two small wiggly eyes to each of the ant heads. Leave to dry. Again, set up a mini production line for each task. Bend the ant legs to give them shape – I use my fingernail to make the initial crease and then pinch and bend to create various leg shapes.

Tip ...

When working with black papers, make sure that your hands are clean, otherwise residues of white glue will show up.

Uplifting Insects

In this comical card, three ants are struggling to hold up the number 18. A hill is cut from pale green card and mounted onto a darker green card blank with foam pads, as in the main design. The impression of juggling movement is achieved by allowing the ant legs to touch and then not touch the hill. The number could be anything from 1 to 80, as all ages will appreciate this design. Alternatively, use it to mark a special (not necessarily wedding) anniversary, such as a garden opening or community project. **Paper lengths:** '1' is made from two lengths, 7cm (23/4in) for the upright and 5cm (2in) for the horizontal; the '0' is made from two 15cm (6in) lengths.

Tip . . .

The letters and numbers don't have to be quilled – you could use ready-made chipboard shapes instead.

Finishing the card

Using the template on page 59, cut the ant hill from green card, then mount onto a square of pale green card using foam pads – these lift the hill away from the background, thereby creating a shadow and the illusion of space, and making the hill stand out. Use the measurements on page 61 to spell out the 'Happy Birthday' message in quilled letters. Position the finished ants and letters as shown above and then glue in place, with the ant legs glued to the quilled letters in some places. Mount the pale green panel onto a darker green card blank.

Love Bugs

Sometimes a simple 'I love you' message is all that's needed! Here, the word 'love' is replaced with a pretty open scroll heart – see page 15 for the open coils technique. For more realistic ants, tiny feelers can be added to the heads of all the ants, but I have left them out to keep them cute-looking. If you don't have small wiggly eyes, you can make quilled eyes from tiny coils of white paper (see step 1, page 30), or use tiny gemstones instead, as in Dainty Dragonflies, pages 40–41.

Fun *flamingos*

The sight of three vibrant flamingos, easily recognizable by their fabulous pink plumage and stick legs, will immediately evoke the thought of warmer climes and holidays on shores afar. Along with the familiar features just mentioned, the flamingos' distinctive long lean neck and black-tipped bill are also replicated in these quilled forms. Their knobbly long legs, created by simple folding, can be angled in such a way to make the birds appear stationary or about to run and take off in flight. These cards are ideal for wishing somebody get well, bon voyage or a happy birthday.

You will need...

- papers: 2mm (1/16in) pink, ivory, black, yellow
- black pen
- pink chalk and applicator
- card: turquoise
- yellow card blank

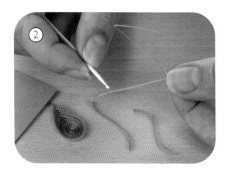

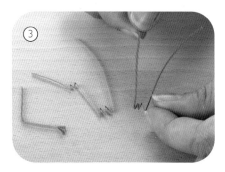

1 For the head of the flamingo, start by joining a 2cm (3/4in) length of black paper end to end to a 5cm (2in) length of yellow. Then join the other end of the yellow paper to a 20cm (8in) length of pink. Starting from the black paper, make a tight coil and glue in place when the end of the yellow is reached, then continue coiling the pink into a loose closed coil. For the bill, make a loose closed coil from a 20cm (8in) length of ivory paper and pinch into a triangle (see page 12). Colour the tip with a black felt-tip pen and the centre with pink chalk.

2 For the body of the flamingo, coil an 80cm (32in) length of pink paper into a loose closed coil and pinch one end to make a teardrop shape (see page 12). Glue to a rectangle of turquoise card. Make another teardrop shape with an 80cm (32in) length of pink paper and glue on top of the first teardrop. To make the flamingo neck, take a 12cm (43/4in) length of pink paper, fold over 4cm (11/2in) along its length and glue, then fold over again and glue. Bend into an 's' shape.

3 Start to make a leg by taking a 15cm (6in) length of pink paper and making a tiny concertina fold 3cm (11/4in) from one end, each fold about 2mm (1/16in). Glue the folds in place. This is the knee. Then make another mini concertina 2.5cm (1in) from the first, apply glue inside each fold and along the length, then press the paper together to create three toes. Finally, glue the pink paper together so that the ends meet. Repeat to make six legs in all.

Fab Flamingo Tag

A single flamingo is mounted onto a tag-shaped piece of turquoise card threaded at the top with narrow blue ribbon. This is then attached with foam pads upright to a tall yellow card blank. A message such as 'Bon voyage' or 'Good luck' could be added. Alternatively, use the flamingo tag on its own to adorn a gift to match the main card.

Tip . . .

If you don't have pink
chalk, you could use a
pale pink felt-tip pen
to colour the flamingos'
bills instead.

Finishing the card

Stick the neck in place on the turquoise card by adding just a small amount
of glue along one edge. Glue the head and beak in position as shown above,
ensuring that they point downwards slightly. Add the legs by gluing them at
the top only and attaching to the underside of the flamingo's body. You can
leave the legs hanging free and bend into shape or add a tiny amount of glue
under the feet to keep them in place. Attach two more flamingos in different
stances so that they are prancing along in a line, then mount the turquoise
card onto a yellow card blank.

Flirtatious Flamingos

This duet of amorous flamingos creates a loving scene, with the birds
standing facing each other, bills almost touching, so that their sinuous necks
suggest a heart shape. For this design, it is essential to make all the elements
of the birds first and then position them without gluing on the heads and
necks, to make sure the placement is correct. This would make an unusual
wedding or anniversary card.

Spiralling *butterflies*

You will need ...

- papers: 3mm (1/8in) deep pink, pale pink, brown, red, orange
- silver glitter glue
- brown paper
- purple card blank
- bright green card

These butterflies are wonderfully dainty and are made by pinning coils to a quilling board, then pinching them into shape. The wings are attached to a rolled body to become freestanding and the butterflies mounted across apertures so that the light shines through their coils to enhance their delicate quality. The use of pink and red papers gives the butterflies extra punch and a touch of glitter on the wing tips added glamour, which makes them especially appealing to youngsters either to make or receive.

1 Glue a 40cm (153/4in) length of deep pink paper end to end to a 20cm (8in) length of pale pink paper. Make a loose closed coil starting with the pale pink paper, then put the coil onto the quilling board. Use a pin to pull the centre of the coil to one edge. Add a dot of glue to the paper near the pin to hold the coil shape in place. Make another spiral the same and then two using a 20cm (8in) length of deep pink glued to a 20cm (8in) length of pale pink paper.

2 When the glue has dried, remove the pin from one coil and gently pinch the coil at the side where the centre of the coil is to make a teardrop shape. Repeat with the other coils. Use a cocktail stick (toothpick) to add silver glitter glue to the tips of the coils. Leave to dry.

3 For the body, cut a triangle from brown paper using the template on page 58. Using a needle tool, start rolling the triangle from the wide end and glue the pointed end in place. Glue the wings to the body. For the antennae, cut a 10cm (4in) length of 3mm (1/8in) brown paper in half lengthways to make a 1.5mm (1/16in) wide strip, then fold in half and coil the ends outwards.

Tip ...

These butterflies could be created using wider paper, such as 5mm (3/16in), and made into hanging decorations.

Butterfly Circle

For a variation, two side-on butterflies feature on the front of this card, with a full-on butterfly on the inside back. Firstly, a circle is cut in a purple card blank and then a printed flower sprig mounted bottom left. Green card is attached to the inside back panel and then a butterfly, made as for the main design, attached. For the other butterflies, just one top and one bottom wing is made for each, plus a body and antennae, again in the same way as for the main card. One butterfly is attached to the circle aperture so that it hangs in the space.

Tip . . .

If you don't have a
quilling board, you could
use a cork board
with circles marked
on instead.

Finishing the card

Make another butterfly the same as the first, then two more using red and orange paper in place of the deep pink and pale pink. Cut four apertures 4cm (1 1/2in) square in a purple card blank, then attach bright green card to the inside back panel of the card. Glue the butterflies across the apertures by adding glue just to the underside of the wing tips. The butterfly bodies could alternatively be made as in step 1, page 18, or you could use loose closed coils pinched flat.

Translucent Butterfly Tag

This is a tag with a difference, using a transparent material – acetate – as an eye-catching background for the butterfly. The acetate is mounted onto a scalloped circle of purple card and then backed with a second circle of card to hide the glue. Complementary-coloured pale green ribbon is threaded through a hole in the top and the butterfly attached with strong glue. The message can then be written on the reverse side in a circle, making a unique gift tag.

Splendid *stork*

To mark such a special occasion as the birth of a baby, it has to be a handmade quilled card! Here, the white stork, long associated with delivering babies, is made using a combination of quilling techniques. Its head is a tight coil formed into a dome and glued inside to hold its shape, with fabulous fluttering eyelashes added. Dangling from its extra-long beak is a sling from which a baby's head and toes peek out. The stork's body and wing consist of large teardrop coils. The main card is clearly for a baby girl, but it can just as easily be made in blue, as in the variation opposite.

You will need ...

- papers: 3mm (1/8in) yellow, white, pink
- card: black, pale pink, pale green
- corner rounder punch
- dark pink card blank
- narrow pink ribbon

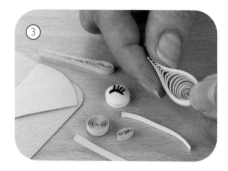

1 For the stork's beak, use a 15cm (6in) length of yellow paper to make a loose closed coil and pinch into a teardrop shape (see page 12). Attach a 20cm (8in) length of yellow paper to the teardrop and loop it around, gradually increasing the size of the loops. Glue the end of the strip in place and then pinch the shape flat.

2 For the stork's head, begin by making a tight coil from an 80cm (32in) length of white paper. Then use your fingers to push the coil into a dome shape. Apply glue to the inside and leave to dry. Cut very tiny strips of black card for the eyelashes and glue to the outside of the dome, using tweezers to position them.

3 Round the corners of a rectangle of pale pink card with a corner rounder punch. For the stork's body, make a 120cm (4ft) length of white paper into a loose closed coil and pinch into a teardrop shape. Glue to the pale pink card. Make a wing from an 80cm (32in) length of white paper also formed into a teardrop and glue on top of the first.

Precious Package Tag

When giving a gift at a baby shower or christening, don't forget to make a matching gift tag! The basis of a pretty tag is quickly created by cutting a scallop-edged circle from dark pink card, which is then threaded with narrow pink ribbon, tied in a bow. A smaller pink circle is then attached to the centre. Here, just the stork's head and beak are all that's needed, with a sling cut from pale pink card and the quilled baby's head and feet added as in the main card. The stork's head and baby sling motif could also be used on any table decorations or for thank you cards.

Tip ...

The eyelashes could be
drawn on with a fine-
tipped black pen to
avoid fiddly cutting
and gluing.

Finishing the card

Make both the stork's neck and leg from a 15cm (6in) length of white paper
folded into three and glued along the length. Attach the head and beak to the
top of the neck. Using the template on page 58, cut a sling from pale green
card and mount onto the pink card with foam pads so that it fits over the
beak. For the baby's head, make a loose closed coil from a 20cm (8in) length
of pink paper and glue to the pink card under the sling. For the baby's feet,
make two pinched coils from 10cm (4in) lengths of pink paper and glue on
the other side of the sling. Mount the pale pink panel onto a dark pink card
blank, also with rounded corners. Cut a notch in the card spine near the
bottom edge, then thread narrow pink ribbon through and tie in a bow.

Double Delivery

This is the perfect card to send to those that have just given birth to twin
boys. The two storks, each dangling a baby, look suitably self-satisfied and
serene in their mission. The storks are made as for the main card and glued
onto an upright rectangle of pale blue card, which is then mounted onto
darker blue card, both again with rounded corners. In this case the storks'
legs are omitted purely for design purposes. A message can be added such
as 'Congratulations' or 'Double trouble'.

Singing *bluebirds*

Miniature bluebirds gather around a handsome nesting box in this lovable card. Two birds are feasting on the hanging nut feeder and its goodies, while another pair are swooping in to join the fun. Each bird consists of coiled and pinched parts, assembled with a looped strip for its tail feathers. The quilled musical notes across the top of the card convey the atmospheric, uplifting sound of bird song. These delightful designs are ideal for new home or housewarming cards.

You will need...

- papers: 2mm (1/16in) pale blue, orange, dark blue, browns, black
- card: pale blue, deep blue, black, brown
- small heart punch
- pattern-edged scissors
- white card blank
- blue string
- die cutter

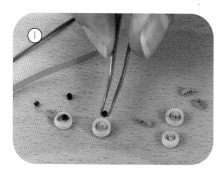

1 For the bird's head, form a 15cm (6in) length of pale blue paper into a loose closed coil. For the beak, make a 3cm (11/4in) length of orange paper into a loose closed coil and pinch into a triangle (see page 12), then attach to the head. For the eye, make a tight closed coil from the narrowest strip of dark blue paper you can coil – I used a 2cm (3/4in) length of 2mm (1/16in) dark blue paper cut in half lengthways. Glue to the head using tweezers to position in place.

2 For the bird's body, form the upper part from a 15cm (6in) length of dark blue paper made into a loose closed coil and pinched into a crescent shape (see page 13) and the lower part using a 20cm (8in) length of pale blue paper, again pinched into a crescent shape. For the wing, coil and pinch a 20cm (8in) length of dark blue paper into a long teardrop shape (see page 12).

3 For the bird's tail, take a 7cm (23/4in) length of dark blue paper and make a large central loop and then two shorter loops either side. Glue the end in place. Glue the tail to the flat side of the body crescent shapes to create one assembled body part. Glue on the head, then attach the wing on top of the lower part of the body.

Tip ...

These bluebirds would also look good when made in other colours, such as yellow and blue for a blue tit or all black for a blackbird.

Homing Birds

For this quicker version of the main card, the nut feeder and stand have been omitted to leave just the nesting box. Five bluebirds are made from aqua and dark blue papers and attached around the box. 'New Home' is printed out on white card, cut into a banner shape and mounted with a foam pad. A bird is glued either side so that their beaks touch the banner, as if they are holding it in place. To save even more time, use only three birds, two for the banner and one on the nesting box.

Tip . . .

For a quicker alternative,
you could use a black
felt-tip pen to draw on
the musical notes
instead of quilling them.

Finishing the card

Use the template on page 58 to cut a nesting box from pale blue card, then
cut out the aperture with a small heart punch. Using pattern-edged scissors,
cut a strip of deep blue card and attach for the box roof, as shown above.
Mount black card to the box back with a foam pad, then glue to a white card
blank. Attach two strips of brown card under the nesting box, horizontally
and vertically, then a small length of blue string to the underside of the box.
Use a die cutter to make a scalloped frame from deep blue card and attach
to the white card. Glue the birds in position. Make feet for two birds (see
step 3, page 54). For the nuts, form 2cm (3/4in) lengths of brown papers into
tight coils and glue in place. For the musical notes, coil 5cm (2in) lengths of
black paper as shown and attach.

Nesting Instinct

This design would again be suitable for a new home, but with the obviously
hungry chicks, it could be to celebrate the arrival of a new addition to an
already large brood! The branch from the Graduation Owl card on pages
48–49 (template on page 59) is used to hold up a nest made from raffia.
The bird's head and body only are used for the chicks that sit in the nest,
angled up towards the parent birds overhead in their eagerness to be fed.
The nesting box is added bottom right, with a bird's head peeping out of
the aperture.

Buzzing *bees*

The bright pinks and oranges of this card make a dynamic backdrop to the realistic, three-dimensional bees buzzing around. The bees are created using a technique that is a bit challenging at first but worth mastering, as it has many other applications. The body of the bees is created in two parts and then joined together to form a round bullet shape. Looping is used to make the delicate wings and wiggly eyes give the bees personality. If you look closely, you will see two types of bee, one with more yellow than black and vice versa.

You will need…

- papers: 3mm (1/8in) black, yellow, white
- 10 small wiggly eyes
- card: pink, pale pink, orange
- narrow orange organza ribbon
- 'Happy Birthday' peel-off sticker
- orange card blank

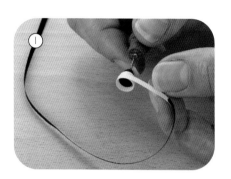

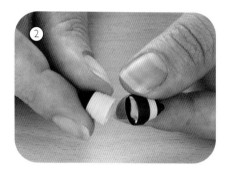

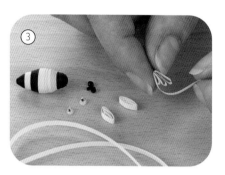

1 For the tail half of all five bee body cones, glue a 30cm (12in) length of black paper end to end to a 15cm (6in) length of yellow and then to a 25cm (10in) length of black paper, making a single length of 70cm (28in). Start coiling from the 30cm (12in) length of black paper and coil tightly for five turns, then angle the paper away from the quilling tool and continue to turn the tool until a cone shape is formed. Continue coiling to the end of the second black strip, then remove the tool. Apply glue to the inside of the cone shape.

2 First make a head half using a 40cm (153/4in) length of black glued to a 40cm (153/4in) length of yellow paper as in step 1. Apply glue to the inside of the cone and fit to a tail half body cone. Repeat to make two more bees in the same way.

3 Now make two more bees but using a 40cm (153/4in) length of black glued to a 20cm (8in) length of yellow paper for the head halves. Make four wings of two sizes for each bee. The top wing is slightly larger, using a 7cm (23/4in) length of white paper looped three times and then wrapped all the way around and the end glued in place. The lower wings are made in the same way but using 6cm (23/8in) lengths of white paper.

Sentiment Suggestions

Buzz round to me soon
Bee mine!
Have a buzzing birthday
To a busy bee!

Bee Happy

Two bees are dangling on clear thread, suspended in an aperture, to give a very realistic 'buzz' to this card! First, a circle aperture is cut in an orange card blank, with pink card mounted onto the inside back panel. Strips of pink card are glued across the front of the card and a mini tag mounted with foam pads top left. The tag is threaded with narrow orange organza ribbon and the message 'bee happy' added. The bees are made in the same way as for the main design, with the clear thread attached to them at step 2. The other end of the thread is glued inside the card. Finally, a bee is glued to the front.

Tip . . .

If you can't get the hang of the coiling cone technique, you can make a flat tight coil and push it out with your fingers, as in step 2, page 28.

Finishing the card

Glue the wings to each bee, along with two small wiggly eyes. Make small antennae for each by folding a 2.5cm (1in) length of black paper in half and coiling the ends outwards. Glue to the middle of the head, at the top of the eyes. Attach horizontal bands of pink and pale pink card of varying widths to an orange card blank, as shown above. Tie narrow orange organza ribbon around the spine of the card ending in a bow at the top. Add a 'Happy Birthday' peel-off sticker to the centre of the card, then glue three bees in a row at the top of the card and two under the message.

Bee Well

This cheerful card will brighten anyone's day, especially if they are feeling a little off-colour. An orange tag tied with orange organza ribbon in a bow has two bees buzzing about on the front around the message 'Get Well Soon'. The tag is mounted with foam pads to pink patterned card, which in turn is glued to a pink card blank with a contrasting stripy inside. Finally, more of the orange ribbon is threaded through two holes made in the spine of the card and tied in a bow.

Peacock *plumage*

The peacock has to be one of the most wonderful display birds, proudly showing off its iridescent tail feathers in a perfect arc. The rich greens and blues of the 'eyes' in its plumage are captured here by using special quilling papers with a metallic edge. As the light catches the metallic colours, the peacock comes to life. Routine coiling and pinching techniques are used for the main card, but it is undeniably labour intensive, so I have included two quick variations.

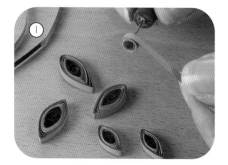

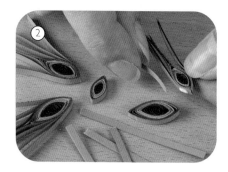

1 There are two sizes of eye feather, and each uses four paper colours. Start by gluing a 10cm (4in) length of blue/metallic blue paper end to end to a 10cm (4in) length of pale blue paper, then to a 15cm (6in) length of mustard paper and finally to a 20cm (8in) length of green/metallic green paper. Insert the blue/metallic blue paper end into the quilling tool and coil to the very end of the green/metallic green paper to make a loose closed coil. For the smaller eye feather, halve all these measurements.

2 Repeat to make a total of 18 larger eye feathers and eight smaller. Glue about eight short lengths of green/metallic green papers, varying in size from 3cm (11/4in) to 5cm (2in), onto each eye, four on each side.

3 For the body, make two 50cm (20in) lengths of blue/metallic blue paper each into a loose closed coil, then pinch as shown. For the eye, make a loose closed coil from a 5cm (2in) length of white glued to a 2cm (3/4in) length of black paper, coiling from the black, then coil a 20cm (8in) length, pinch into a crescent shape and wrap around. For the beak, use a tiny piece of white; for the feet, use 5cm (2in) (see step 3, page 54); for the head coils, use 5cm (2in) each of the same blue.

Tip ...

This card design is so sophisticated and stunning that it could be mounted in a frame for permanent display as a picture.

Eye of Wonder

In this single peacock feather design, the fabulous 'eye' of the feather becomes the focus of the card. The large feather is made by multiplying the measurements for the larger eye feathers in step 1 by three, i.e. a 30cm (12in) length of blue/metallic blue paper glued to a 30cm (12in) length of pale blue, then to a 45cm (18in) length of mustard and finally to a 40cm (153/4in) length of green/metallic green paper. The neutral nature of this card means that it can be applied to many different occasions, such as for a bereavement or a birthday.

Tip . . .

A lot of metallic-edged
paper is needed for the
main card, so check on
your stocks before
you start.

Finishing the card

Once you have made all the eye feathers, start by gluing seven large feathers
onto a rectangle of pale blue card, beginning at the outer arc to form the
outline shape. Then glue another 11 large feathers under the others to fill in
the tail. Lastly, glue on the eight smaller feathers to create an inner arc. Use
scissors to snip the ends of the green papers on the outer feathers to make
an even yet not too symmetrical shape. Make coils from 10cm (4in) and
15cm (6in) lengths of green paper, then pinch and glue to form a solid block
that will be behind the body. Glue on the body, head and feet. Mount the
panel onto a dark blue card blank.

Feather Fans

For a less time-consuming card, here just three peacock tail feathers are
mounted onto pale blue card. This card or a matching tag could make
creative use of any leftover shapes or miscellaneous pieces from the main
card. The design would work well for wedding invitations or save-the-date
cards. Don't be afraid to use artistic licence and change the colour schemes
of these feathers to, say, purples or all blues. As long as the shape remains
the same, they will remain recognizable as exotic peacock feathers.

Ladybird *cuties*

Ladybirds, or ladybugs, are one of the cutest insects ever and they look extra appealing in quilled form. There are many ways to quill a ladybird and over the years I have experimented a great deal, with these being the product of my latest development. The rounded shape of the body is created by pushing up the centre of a quilled coil to form a dome. Black pen is used to add the bugs' endearing dots and their heads are brought to life with wiggly eyes. Those on the move have tiny quilled legs, while others are made without legs as if resting, just as real ladybirds do!

1 For the largest ladybirds, glue four 40cm (15 3/4in) lengths of 3mm (1/8in) red paper end to end to make one long length. Quill into a tight coil, then use your fingertip to push up the centre of the coil to make an even dome shape. Use a cocktail stick (toothpick) to apply a generous amount of glue inside the dome. Leave to dry. Make more bodies with 120cm (4ft) and 80cm (32in) lengths of red paper for the medium and small ladybirds.

2 For the largest ladybirds, make heads using 40cm (15 3/4in) lengths of 2mm (1/16in) black paper pinched into a crescent shape (see page 13). For the two smaller sizes of ladybird, use 30cm (12in) lengths to make the heads. The antennae are 3cm (1 1/4in) lengths folded in half and the ends coiled outwards. Add small wiggly eyes to the two smaller sizes of ladybird and larger eyes to the largest ladybirds.

3 Use a black felt-tip pen to add random dots to the outside of each body. For the ladybird legs, use 3cm (1 1/4in) lengths of black paper. Coil but stop short of the end, then glue to create a tight coil, leaving a 'tail'. Pinch the coils to flatten. Glue the 'tail' to the inside of the body. Add six legs to each 'walking' ladybird.

Sentiment Suggestions

To my love bug on your birthday

Get the birthday bug today!

Have a wonderful bugday!

Lucky Ladybirds

Here, the lucky number 7 is cut from green card and stamped, as in the main card, but instead of being glued directly to the card it is mounted with foam pads to raise it slightly from the background. The three ladybirds are then balanced along the top of the number. One more ladybird is struggling up the number and one is left behind at the bottom. Finally, two more (to make up a total of seven) nestle together bottom right.

Tip . . .

Instead of using your
fingertip to push up the
tight coils in step 1, you
could use a pen top
or glue lid.

Finishing the card

Using the templates on page 60, cut a number 1 and 0 from bright green card. Print over the numbers with a leaf-patterned rubber stamp and a green ink pad to create a subtle foliage effect. Glue the numbers to a dark green card blank. Attach a strip of matching green leaf-stamped paper across the bottom of the card and add a 'Happy Birthday' rub-on greeting. Glue on the ladybirds – I used 10 in all, some with legs and some 'resting' (without legs) – to decorate the numbers.

Snuggle Bugs

Any child just turning three years old will love this adorable card, with resting ladybirds snuggled in the curves of the number. The number 3 is cut from green card and stamped, as for the main card, then mounted onto a dark green circle card with foam pads. The ladybirds are in each of the three sizes to make a family, and glued directly to the card. Do take care when sending cards to young children – it's a good idea to put a warning to parents on the card of any choking hazard.

Partridge *in a pear tree*

You will need…

- papers: 3mm (1/8in) black, brown, pale brown, dark brown, gold-edged brown, dark green, yellow
- card: cream, brown
- dark green card blank

'On the first day of Christmas my true love gave to me a partridge in a pear tree', as the well-known festive song begins. Here, a plump partridge is prettily perched amidst quilled leaves and pears to create a special card for Christmas. To make the partridge shine out, paper edged with gold is used for the bird's wing and tail, while different shades of brown paper bring a subtle colour variation and visual interest to the plumage. The tree is constructed with gracefully flowing branches of deep green leaves, laden with luscious, golden pears.

1 For the partridge's head, glue a 5cm (2in) length of black paper end to end to a 40cm (15 3/4in) length of brown. Put the black paper into the quilling tool and make a tight coil, glue and then continue to coil to make a loose closed coil with the brown. For the beak, use a 6cm (2 3/8in) length of brown paper to make a tight coil and pinch flat, then join to a flattened coil made with a 3cm (1 1/4in) length.

2 For the central part of the partridge's body, use an 80cm (32in) length of pale brown paper to make a loose closed coil. Then make two more coils, each using 40cm (15 3/4in) lengths of dark brown, and pinch into crescent shapes (see page 13). Glue either side of the central body part. Make a wing from a 60cm (23 3/4in) length of gold-edged brown paper pinched into a teardrop shape (see page 12). Finally, for the tail, use a 9cm (3 1/2in) length of the same paper looped five times into a fan shape.

3 For the tree branches, glue 20cm (8in) and 15cm (6in) lengths of dark green paper together at one end to form the trunk. Position on a square of cream card and trim the lengths to suit. Add two smaller branches, as shown in the photo opposite. Make the leaves from 20cm (8in) lengths of the dark green paper, then pinch into eye shapes (see page 12). For the pears, use 20cm (8in) lengths of yellow paper to make coils, then gently pinch into pear shapes with a loop at the top.

Sentiment Suggestions

Thinking of you this Christmas
'Tis the season to be jolly
Sending you Peace and Joy
Merry Christmas

Partridge Perfect

This design sits the partridge on a branch with only three pears for a quicker version of the main card involving less quilling. The bird is made from plain papers without a gold edge to show how it can still work well without the gilding. 'Season's Greetings' is printed onto card and then mounted using foam pads. The branches flow under the greeting to integrate it into the overall design.

Tip . . .

If you don't have gold-edged brown paper, plain brown paper will also look good.

Finishing the card

It's best to position the partridge on the main branch first and then glue the five pears around so that they are evenly spaced. Then add the leaves to all the branches as shown above. Here, the leaves are fairly loosely spaced so that the card doesn't become too cluttered, but you can add as many or as few as you wish. A festive greeting could be added if a space was left bottom right on the card. Mount the cream panel onto brown card and then onto a dark green card blank.

Partridge in a Heart Tree

For this card, the branches are shaped as if in a topiary to form a heart that envelopes the partridge. Two lengths of green paper are glued together at one end and then the paper curled up and over for the heart frame. The five pears are then added followed by the leaves. Some leaves are glued on their side to vary the texture of the branches. Finally, the partridge is placed in the centre. A message could be added such as 'with love at Christmastime'.

Dainty *dragonflies*

Dragonflies are beautiful creatures, with bright bodies and delicate wings. In fact, their wings are so fine and beat so fast that only their bodies are seen clearly when they whiz by. Here, closed coils used to create the bodies are painted for a shimmering effect and the delicate wings made using a looping and wrapping technique. The finished dragonflies are then set against a rubber-stamped background to give the impression of foliage. The main design features the popular 'easel' style of card.

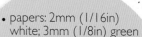
You will need...

- papers: 2mm (1/16in) white; 3mm (1/8in) green
- rubber stamps: floral, script
- ink pads: greens
- card: pale turquoise, dark turquoise
- shimmer paint and fine
- paintbrush
- 4 tiny gemstones
- tag punch
- green brad

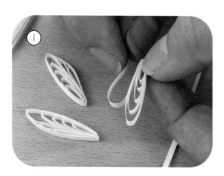

1 For a dragonfly wing, take a 35cm (13¾in) length of 2mm (1/16in) white paper and bend over one end about 1cm (3/8in). Loop the paper around to create a second loop, larger than the first. Continue looping five times until the shape measures 2.5cm (1in) in length. Create a loop along one side of the main one and a second smaller loop, wrap the paper around the whole shape and glue the end in place. If you have excess paper, trim the end. Make three more wings in this way, making sure they are the same size.

2 For the dragonfly body, make eight loose closed coils from two 15cm (6in), one 10cm (4in) and five 5cm (2in) lengths of 3mm (1/8in) green paper. Glue together the two 15cm (6in) coils to form the head of the dragonfly, then pinch the 10cm (4in) coil into a long triangle (see page 12) and glue beneath. Pinch the 5cm (2in) coils into tiny triangles. Stamp pale turquoise card with the floral and script designs using green inks, then glue the pinched shapes in a line as shown.

3 Glue the wings either side of the body so that they touch the second large coil. Dip a fine paintbrush into water and then rub on the solid shimmer paint to pick up the colour. Paint the top of each coil with the colour. Leave to dry.

Captured Beauty

To send congratulations on a new home, a single dragonfly is set within a square frame. Firstly, the dragonfly is glued to a pale green card blank that has been subtly stamped with a floral pattern. A darker green frame is cut and also stamped with floral and script stamps. The frame is then attached, using foam pads, onto the card with the dragonfly. The 'New Home' message is printed onto a mini tag and a brad inserted. This is mounted bottom left with a foam pad.

Tip . . .

The shimmer paint on the dragonfly
bodies adds the finishing touch but
can be omitted as a short cut.
Alternatively, quilling papers with a
metallic edge could be used.

Finishing the card

Add two tiny gemstones to the dragonfly for eyes. Make a second dragonfly
and position below the first. Mount the card panel onto an easel card made
from dark turquoise card. Cut a narrow strip and punch a mini tag shape
from matching stamped card. Attach the strip to a slightly wider strip of dark
turquoise card and secure the tag to this with a green brad. Add a message
such as 'Love' to the tag. Instead of stamping the card, you could use a bought
sheet of card ready-printed with a pattern to save time or if you don't have
the necessary rubber stamps.

Flight of Fancy

A whirlwind of hovering dragonflies has been created for this pretty, animated
card. Three dragonflies with green bodies adorn the upper part of the card,
while two with blue bodies are featured in the offset rectangle. When featuring
several dragonflies, don't make the composition too symmetrical or it will lose
the natural quality of the subject matter. Two dragonflies overlap top left, with
the wings of one resting above the other – if you don't feel confident, make the
dragonflies separately and then position on the card. This design will take more
time but has lots of uses, such as for a fifth wedding anniversary, a retirement or
a special birthday.

Elegant *swans*

A pair of graceful swans set against a dark blue background creates a simple yet striking design. An unusual tool is put to good use to create the swans' wings. The paper strips are threaded through and around an onion holder/slicer for a technique quillers call 'spreuers'. The wide prongs of this comb-like tool are ideal for threading and looping paper strips, gluing in place and then sliding off. The resulting shape is different to traditional quilling, as the flat side of the papers are facing rather than coils on their edge. Both techniques are combined here.

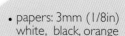

You will need ...

- papers: 3mm (1/8in) white, black, orange
- deep blue card
- 2 small black gemstones
- onion holder or similar
- deep blue card blank

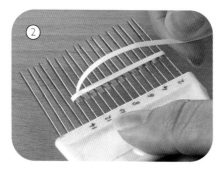

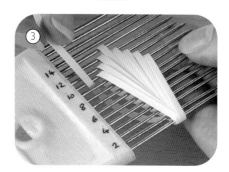

1 For the swan body, coil an 80cm (32in) length of white paper into a loose closed coil. Pinch one end and then glue in place on a long, narrow rectangle of deep blue card. Use another 80cm (32in) length for the neck of the swan, pinching one end of the coil very flat and bending the other end over and pushing it in. Make the beak in two parts, using a 10cm (4in) length of black paper coiled and pinched into a crescent shape (see page 13) and a 10cm (4in) length of orange paper coiled and pinched into a narrow teardrop (see page 12). For the eye, attach a small black gemstone to the white coil.

2 Take a 40cm (15 3/4in) length of white paper and thread the paper around the onion holder at rung 14 from the bottom (the number will vary according to what type of onion holder is used), then glue the end in place on the reverse side to create a loop. This is the centre loop. Now take the end of the paper and thread through the gap between rung 14 and 13, then glue in place on the reverse side at the bottom rung.

3 Thread the end of the paper between rung 14 and 13 on the other side of the centre loop so that the shape becomes symmetrical. Continue threading and looping either side of the centre loop, decreasing by one prong each time, stopping at rung 7 on the right-hand side and prong 8 on the other. At some point you will need to glue another 40cm (15 3/4in) length to the end of the first.

Sedate Swan

A single swan is just as elegant but less obviously romantic, so ideal for a card for any occasion. The swan is made as for the main card, and this design could easily be adapted to create a matching gift tag or a place setting. Cygnets (young swans) can also be quilled to accompany the adult swan, made from grey paper for a realistic effect. You could even add tiny cygnets to the back of the swan, as they hitch a ride on a parent, for a new baby card. The swan could alternatively be made using black papers for a different look.

Finishing the card

Glue both swan bodies and necks on first so that the heads are close but not touching. Then make a single wing following steps 2 and 3 opposite and then glue to the swan on the left of the card. Make another wing but this time stop the looping at rung 7 on the left-hand side and prong 8 on the other so that the wings are not exactly symmetrical in themselves but each swan is a mirror image of the other. Mount the blue card panel onto a deep blue card blank with foam pads. A greeting could be added if it's for an anniversary or wedding.

Swan Skimming

With their long necks, swans can reach down into the water to find food, and here the swan is skimming the surface for edible algae. To begin with, a swan body and neck are made as for the main card, but when the neck is glued on the card it is arced downwards with the beak below the body line. A strip of card with a wavy top edge is layered across the base of the card using foam pads so that it stands proud and just covers the swan's beak and the bottom of its body, to give the impression of the water's surface.

Dazzling *butterfly*

When quilled coils are glued together en masse, they can be very robust, as demonstrated in this gorgeous 3D butterfly. The two ornate wings are angled against the small body and float in the air, making the effect even more realistic. When working on a larger project like this, a good system is to gradually build up each wing, starting at the base and working outwards to the tips. To avoid frustrating and time-consuming measuring, all the wing coils use either 10cm (4in) or 20cm (8in) lengths of paper in just three colours.

You will need...

- papers: 3mm (1/8in) pale orange, brown, orange
- card: turquoise, pale turquoise
- acetate (optional)

1 For the top wing, start by making four coils from 20cm (8in) lengths of pale orange paper and pinch into teardrop shapes (see page 12). Glue together to form a block. Make two tight coils from 10cm (4in) lengths of brown paper, then glue to the block of four. Make three teardrop shapes from 10cm (4in) lengths of orange paper and then one eye shape (see page 12) from a 20cm (8in) length of orange paper.

2 Make 12 teardrop shapes from 10cm (4in) lengths of orange and three from pale orange paper, then three loose closed coils from brown paper. Build up the wing by adding the shapes as shown.

3 Wrap a length of brown paper around each wing to assist the structure and keep the coils together. The lower wing consists of three pale orange eye shapes and two brown tight coils made from 20cm (8in) lengths, plus 10 orange loose closed coils made from 10cm (4in) lengths. The feature of the lower wing is the teardrop shape, which is made from a 10cm (4in) length of brown paper glued end to end to a 20cm (8in) length of pale orange. Starting from the brown, make into a loose closed coil, then gently pinch into a teardrop.

Tip ...

Here I have used 3mm (1/8in) paper, but you could use 5mm (3/16in) paper instead for a stronger structure.

Fabulously Framed

This interesting window tag design features a smaller 3D butterfly made by reducing the number of coils. The top and lower wings begin with the same measurements as the main card but then the two outermost layers on the top wing and one outer layer on the lower wing are omitted. A strip of pale blue card is cut along one edge with pattern-edged scissors and mounted to the bottom edge of a tag shape cut from darker blue card, which is then threaded with strands of ribbon in colours to match the butterfly. The quilled motif is glued to the tag, then mounted at an angle within a box frame card.

Tip . . .

You can use a quilling board
to make sure that your
coiled shapes are evenly
sized. The butterfly could be
mounted onto a thin stick
and used as a decoration.

Finishing the card

For the butterfly body, make a loose closed coil from a 40cm (15 3/4in) length
of brown paper and pinch tightly at one end. For the antennae, fold a 10cm
(4in) length of brown paper in half and coil each end away from the fold
with a needle tool. Make a box frame card from turquoise card with pale
turquoise card mounted in the back of the box. Glue the butterfly inside
so that the wings are 'fluttering' but protected by the card. If the butterfly
structure isn't strong enough, add a strip of acetate behind the butterfly and
glue to the body.

Fluttering By

Equally effective is this butterfly with just one top and one lower wing to
create a side-on view. It is glued to a turquoise card, which is then mounted
onto a pale turquoise card blank. A notch is cut in the spine of the card near
the bottom edge and orange organza ribbon threaded through. This could be
used as a get well or a 'thinking of you' card. The colour scheme of the
butterfly can be easily changed to use whatever you have in your paper stock,
but make sure you choose a complimentary colour for the background and
card blank as here.

Friendly *penguins*

These jolly penguins are all sending festive greetings and looking very cute too! A paper crimper is used to crinkle the paper strips before coiling to create an interesting texture and a suitably wintry 'shivery' effect. Otherwise, the usual coiling and pinching is used. The eyes of the penguins are simply open circles of white paper, but they are very effective when set against the black of the heads. The penguins are of different sizes in the main design to make a family group, but the one far right is wobbling, on the slide and about to fall off, as in a real-life family photo!

You will need...

- papers: 3mm (1/8in) black, white; 2mm (1/16in) orange, white
- paper crimper
- red card
- 'Happy Christmas' peel-off sticker
- green striped paper
- red card blank

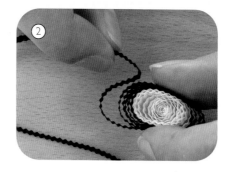

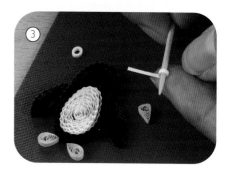

1 Use the crimper to crinkle strips of 3mm (1/8in) black and white papers by turning the cogs, forcing the paper through. All the penguins use a 40cm (153/4in) length of crimped white paper joined end to end to the same length of crimped black paper. Use the quilling tool to form the joined strips into a loose closed coil.

2 For the larger penguin, take another 40cm (153/4in) length of crimped black paper and attach to the body on one side. Loosely fold the paper over the top to the other side and back again. Continue until you reach the end of the paper. Glue to a rectangle of red card.

3 Make two wings each using a 15cm (6in) length of crimped black paper. Attach either side. The nose (beak) and feet are all made from 8cm (31/4in) lengths of 2mm (1/6in) orange paper; and the eyes are formed using 6cm (23/8in) lengths of 2mm (1/16in) white paper rolled around a cocktail stick (toothpick).

Sentiment Suggestions

Chill out this Christmas
Sending you festive love
Have a cool Christmas

Penguin Pair

Two penguins of different sizes hold hands in this endearing design. The square of red card is mounted onto a narrow, folded piece of pink card. This card would be ideal for giving to a sweetheart with a message such as 'with love at Christmas', or you could use it instead to mark a wedding anniversary. Quilled hearts could be added (see Love Birds, page 21) for an extra romantic touch.

Tip . . .

If you don't have a
crimper tool to make
the crinkled paper, you
can simply use
uncrimped paper.

Finishing the card

Cut a strip of wavy red card and mount below the penguin with foam pads so
that the penguin feet just touch the raised card. Attach a 'Happy Christmas' peel-
off sticker to green striped paper and cut out in a banner shape. Mount onto
the centre of the red card with foam pads. Make two more penguins the same
size and attach. For the smaller penguin, use a 20cm (8in) length of crimped
black paper for looping over the head and make the wings using 10cm (4in)
lengths of the paper, but all the other measurements are the same. Glue green
striped paper to a red card blank card with the fold at the top, then attach the
red card penguin panel across the centre so that it protrudes a little either side.

Penguin Gang

Three penguins of the same size stand in line for lots of festive fun. The
penguins are made using the dimensions for the larger penguin and then
glued to a strip of red card. Green striped paper is attached to a pink card
blank with the fold at the top, onto which the red card penguin panel is
mounted with foam pads so that the ends protrude slightly as in the main
design. Finally, a 'Christmas' peel-off stick is added below the penguin line-up.

Graduation *owl*

The wise old owl is a well-known symbol of knowledge and learning, and is therefore ideally suited to a graduation card or exam success. This quilled owl is created using a combination of different quilled coils and shapes in varying shades of brown. The brainy bird is appropriately crowned with a black graduation hat (mortarboard), fitted neatly on its head, complete with a fringed tassel. The two variation cards show how to make a smaller owl and also larger eyes for an alternative owlish expression.

You will need …

- papers: 3mm (1/8in) black, white, browns; 10mm (3/8in) black
- paper: cream, brown textured, script-patterned
- black embroidery thread
- black card
- gold card blank

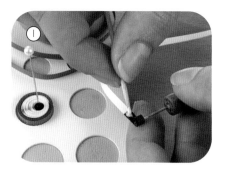

1 Each eye consists of a 10cm (4in) length of 3mm (1/8in) black paper glued end to end to a 40cm (15³/4in) length of white paper and then to the same length of brown paper. Start coiling from the black paper and make a tight coil, glue to secure and then continue quilling to the end of the entire length to make a loose closed coil. Put onto a quilling board, then use a pin to pull the centre to one side and glue in place.

2 Start building the owl by gluing the eyes in place on a rectangle of cream paper with torn edges. Make loose closed coils from 60cm (23³/4in) lengths of dark brown paper, then pinch into narrow crescents, as shown, and glue down from the eyes. Hold in place while the glue dries. Add another outer crescent coil to each side each made using a 40cm (15³/4in) length of dark brown paper. Then make about 15 coils using 15cm (6in) lengths of paler brown paper and pinch to fit together and fill in the body.

3 Use a fringing tool to cut a 10cm (4in) length of 10mm (3/8in) black paper. Glue a 5cm (2in) piece of black embroidery thread to the uncut part of the fringed paper and then start coiling. Using the templates on page 59, cut the two pieces for the graduation hat (mortarboard) from black card. Glue together, as shown in the photo opposite, with the end of the tassel glued to the reverse side.

Rewarding Owlet

This cute little learned chap is flying off to deliver an important document – probably an exam certificate! The owl is made smaller by starting with the eyes, again glued at an angle in this case onto mauve paper, but this time the outer crescents are omitted and just nine pinched shapes used for the body. Each wing comprises three 15cm (6in) lengths of dark brown paper, coiled and pinched into narrow eye shapes, then glued together either side of the body. The hat, beak and claws are made as for the main card. A small piece of cream paper is rolled and tied with red ribbon, then glued below the claws.

Tip . . .

If you find making
quilled eyes a bit tricky,
why not use large
wiggly eyes instead.

Finishing the card

For the beak, use a 20cm (8in) length of dark brown paper to make a loose closed coil, then pinch into a diamond shape (see page 13). Using the template on page 59, cut the branch from brown textured paper, then glue below the owl. Mount the cream paper onto a rectangle of script-patterned paper and then onto a mauve card blank. Make each of the two claws from three 5cm (2in) lengths of brown paper, formed into tight coils, pinched flat and glued together. Glue these on last, on top of the branch. You could also add a greeting, such as 'Congratulations!' or 'Well done'. This design is perfect for adapting to make a Harry Potter-style card for a Hogwarts enthusiast.

Guardian Owl

This thoughtful owl is looking upwards with large, round watchful eyes. It is easy to make eyes of different sizes by adding or removing lengths of paper. These are made using a 10cm (4in) length of black paper glued to an 80cm (32in) length of white and then to a 40cm (15 3/4in) length of brown, coiled starting from the black paper. Instead of a graduation hat, a 40cm (15 3/4in) length of brown paper is pinched into a crescent shape and then glued above the eyes. One set of outer wings is attached and then filled in with 11 coils of paler brown paper. A message could be added such as 'Good luck!'.

Bejewelled *butterfly*

A variation on the traditional rolling and coiling of papers is to wrap the paper strips around pins, known as the 'husking' technique, used here to create intricate butterflies. After wrapping and gluing the strips of paper, the pins are removed and the looped shape glued directly to card and cut out, as in the main design, or glued across an aperture, as in the variation below. The loops can be filled in with open or closed coils, or enhanced with gemstones or other embellishments as desired.

You will need...

- papers: 3mm (1/8in) pinks, purple
- foam board and pins
- masking tape
- card: pink, mauve
- purple card blank
- 2 small and 8 large
- gemstones

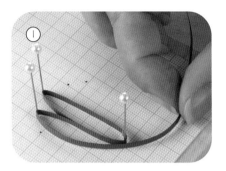

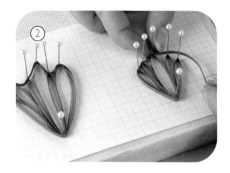

1 Trace or photocopy the template on page 61 onto paper. Place on a foam board and secure with masking tape. For the lower wing, insert a pin through the paper and into the foam board at the points marked 1 and 2. Take a length of pink paper and wrap around pins 1 and 2 to create a loop, then glue the end in place. Insert another pin at the point marked 3, then take the paper up and around the pin.

2 Continue to insert pins, following the numbered sequence, and loop the paper around the pins as shown. Finally, take the paper around the outside of the shape, glue in place and use your fingers to press the paper inwards. This photo shows the top wing complete and the lower wing being completed.

3 Glue the top and lower wing to pink card. Make a body from a 40cm (15 3/4in) length of pink paper pinched into a long, narrow teardrop shape (see page 12). Glue to the pink card. Make another top and lower wing to match. Using small scissors, cut out around the outer edge of the butterfly shape.

Lace-Winged Window

Once again the robustness of quilled strips is demonstrated here by attaching the lace-like wings of a husking butterfly across a circular aperture. Just the tips of the two wings are glued to the card to hold it in place. The body is glued to the wings and then the coils adhered inside the shape. It's important to apply glue around the edge of the pinched coils only so that they will stick to the loops of the wings. A greeting is added to a circle of matching card and mounted top left.

Have a Wonderful Day

Tip . . .

It's easy to make smaller
butterflies using the
husking technique just
by moving the pins
inwards to create
smaller loops.

Finishing the card

Glue the butterfly to a purple card blank at an angle so that half is above the
top edge. Add two small gemstones to the top of the body for eyes. For
antennae, fold a 10cm (4in) length of paper in half and coil the ends
outwards. Make eight teardrop shapes from 20cm (8in) lengths of purple
paper and glue to the wing tips, inside the husking shape. Make two open
coils with 20cm (8in) lengths of pink paper and glue to the top wings as
shown above – make sure you keep the decoration symmetrical. Add large
gemstones to the pinched coils. Attach a strip of mauve card across the
bottom of the card blank, with a narrower strip of pink card on top, then a
length of pink quilling paper. Add a greeting if you wish.

Tranquil Butterfly

For a quicker version of the main card, only one top and one lower wing are
made to create the calming image of a resting butterfly. All the measurements
are the same as those for the main card. For the butterfly legs, three small
pieces of paper are attached to the body and then some folds added. The
colour scheme of the butterfly can be easily changed to suit the recipient,
for example oranges and browns as used in Dazzling Butterfly, pages 44–45,
or blues and blacks for a dramatic effect.

Spooky *spider*

Spiders are an essential part of the Halloween festivities and this three-dimensional quilled one is amazingly realistic. The spider's characteristic long, segmented legs are created by attaching pinched coils end to end. The eight legs are glued to a convincingly domed body, with small pincers adding a final creepy touch. Just the tips of the dreaded insect's legs are attached to the card so that it stands proud, as if to run away! In fact, it doesn't have to be on a card at all, just left around the house to scare the unsuspecting.

1 Glue four 40cm (153/4in) lengths of 3mm (1/8in) black paper end to end to make a 160cm (63in) length, then form into a tight coil. Push the centre of the coil up with your fingertips to make a dome shape. Use a cocktail stick (toothpick) to apply a generous amount of glue inside the dome. Leave to dry. Create another dome shape with three 40cm (153/4in) lengths glued end to end to make a 120cm (4ft) length. For the pincers, use two 10cm (4in) lengths of 2mm (1/16in) black paper, form each into a loose closed coil and pinch into a crescent shape (see page 13).

2 For each identical leg, make loose closed coils from one 20cm (8in) length and four 10cm (4in) lengths of 3mm (1/8in) black paper, then pinch into eye shapes. Glue them end to end, starting with the large pinched coil, on acetate, positioning them angled as shown. Leave the glue to dry completely.

3 Glue the head, body and pincers together, then sit the assembled parts on a small object to elevate it from the work surface, such as an eraser. Take a leg, put glue on the large pinched coil end and stick to the spider's head. Glue four legs either side and leave to dry.

Tip...

For arachnophobes, make the spiders more fun-looking by adding wiggly eyes or use coloured papers such as purple instead of black.

Scary Sentiment

For many, the scary part of the spider is its long legs, so here they are made shorter by using only four pinched coils per leg. The rest of the spider is made as for the main card. A quarter cobweb shape is cut from bright green card and the cobweb drawn on with orange glitter glue. This is then mounted onto black card once the glue is dry. The corners of an orange card blank are rounded and the cobweb mounted onto the front. The cobweb shape is then cut from the front panel and the spider attached to the cobweb. A 'Booooo' and bat peel-off stickers are added to the back panel of the card for the finishing touch.

Tip ...

Why not make all three
sizes of spider for a
Halloween display –
you could add a length of
thread to each body
to suspend them.

Finishing the card

Cut a triangle of orange card large enough for the spider and then draw on
a cobweb with silver glitter glue. Leave to dry. Mount onto a slightly larger
triangle of purple card and then onto a bright green triangle card blank. Glue
the spider to the cobweb by just adding a dot of glue under six of the feet,
positioning it so that the spider's feet touch part of the cobweb but leave
two feet free and unglued – it will look odd if the feet don't touch the
cobweb. You could leave a space for a message, such as 'Happy Halloween'.

Cuddly Spider

For a slightly cuter spider, just make it smaller! Here, a tight coil is made with
a 120cm (4ft) length of 3mm (1/8in) black paper, then pushed up to make a
dome and glued inside, as for the main card. Two pincers are made and
attached as before, but only one large and two small pinched coils are used
for each leg. A complete cobweb shape is cut from orange card and then
silver glitter glue used to draw on the cobweb, including a deliberate tear.
The cobweb is then mounted onto a round purple card blank and finally the
spider glued in place on the web.

Swooping *seagulls*

Swooping and diving seagulls are the feature of these action-packed quilled card designs. The wings are angled in shape and shaded with paint to give the impression of movement and flight. Combined with long legs in varying positions, the birds look either like they have just taken off or are about to make a landing. The nautical theme is emphasized in the main card by the red flag-shaped card blank, eyelets and cord tied around the spine, which is carried through in the two variation cards. These designs are ideal for men and boys.

You will need...

- papers: 3mm (1/8in) white, black, orange
- grey ink pad
- sheet of foil
- paintbrush
- blue card
- eyelets and eyelet setting kit
- red card blank
- blue cord

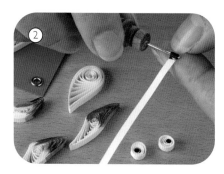

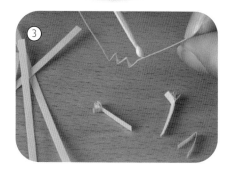

1 For each seagull wing, use a 40cm (15 3/4in) length of white paper to make a loose closed coil, then pinch and bend almost into a 'z' shape, as shown. Press a grey ink pad onto a sheet of foil to leave a residue of ink. Rub a damp paintbrush onto the ink to collect colour, then paint the tips of the wings.

2 For the seagull body, use a 40cm (15 3/4in) length of white paper to make a loose closed coil, then pinch into a teardrop shape (see page 13). Glue in place on a rectangle of blue card, with eyelets set in each corner. For the seagull head, glue a 2cm (3/4in) length of black paper end to end to a 10cm (4in) length of white. Start coiling from the black paper and then glue at the end of the black paper to form a tight coil. Continue coiling to form a loose closed coil with the white paper.

3 For each leg, take a 5cm (2in) length of orange paper, make a tiny folded zigzag at the midpoint and put glue inside, then press together to make three feet. Trim the length to suit the bird. For the beak, fold a 1cm (3/8in) length of orange paper in half and glue to the head.

Sentiment Suggestions

Squark! Squark!
We're flying in to see you
Swoop in and visit soon
Have a great flight but
return soon

Seagull Feast

A fish and chip meal is a must-have for most Brits when at the seaside and we usually end up feeding a few gulls as well! Here, two seagulls swoop down on an unattended takeaway in this fun card. The seagulls are mounted onto pale blue card that has had a white ink pad rubbed over it to make light clouds. Brown card becomes a brick wall, on which sits crumpled newspaper (the traditional wrapping for fish and chips). The chips are cut-up strips of yellow foam glued onto the paper. Blue cord is threaded through eyelets along the card base to enhance the nautical feel.

Tip …

Apply the grey colour
sparingly to the quilled
shapes, otherwise the
paper will absorb too
much water and
become soggy.

Finishing the card

Cut a triangle from the right-hand edge of a red card blank, both front and
back panels. Tie a length of blue cord around the spine of the card in a knot
– I have used a reef knot. Here, eyelets have been set in each corner of the
rectangle of blue card, but if you don't have these and an eyelet setting kit,
you could use small metal brads instead. Glue the seagulls at different angles
to the blue card, as shown above, then mount the card onto the red card
blank with foam pads. A message could be added such as 'Bon voyage'
or 'Enjoy your trip'.

To the Lighthouse

A printed lighthouse image is used as a scenic feature around which the
seagulls swoop in this design. The bottom gull is walking along rather than
flying, so only one wing is attached. Quilling can be combined with other
papercrafts, using any interesting paper pieces you might have tucked away in
your paper stash. Here, the nautical chart, for instance, used for layering onto
the card blank to form a decorative border, is a recycled real but out-of-date
chart. Dark blue cord is tied in a simple knot and attached to the bottom of
the card, as well as a short length threaded through eyelets.

Christmas *cardinal*

You will need...

- papers: 3mm (1/8in) red, orange, black, brown; 2mm (1/16in) green
- card: green, cream
- black felt-tip pen
- black bead
- ivory Flower Soft®
- dark green card blank

The red cardinal bird is a fabulous motif for Christmas cards, providing the perfect excuse to indulge in bright colours. The body of the bird is more labour intensive than others in this book, but all the coils are made with 10cm (4in) lengths of quilling paper, so no complicated measuring is needed. The wings and tail feathers are looped strips of red paper joined together to create a lighter effect. The bird stands upon a branch dusted with snow for an extra wintery feel. The variation cards feature cardinals that are slightly smaller and therefore quicker to make.

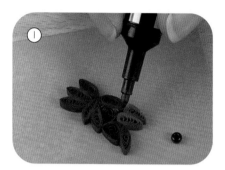

1 Start by forming the head of the red cardinal. Pinch three 10cm (4in) lengths of 3mm (1/8in) red paper into eye shapes for the head feathers (see page 12). Then pinch each of two 10cm (4in) lengths of orange paper into a triangle for the beak. Position these on a rectangle of green card, then add two coils made from 10cm (4in) lengths of black paper in between. Use black felt-tip pen to colour the beak and red coils slightly to make more natural-looking. Add a black bead for the eye.

2 Position a long, slightly wavy length of 2mm (1/16in) green paper as the main branch. For the leaves, make loose closed coils from 20cm (8in) lengths of green paper and pinch into eye shapes. Glue either side of the branch. Make the bird's feet using 6cm (23/8in) lengths of 3mm (1/8in) brown paper (see step 3, page 24) and glue in position. For the body, make coils using 10cm (4in) lengths of red paper.

3 For the wing, take a 40cm (153/4in) length of red paper and make a small loop, then make another larger loop. Continue looping, gradually increasing the size of the loop, until you reach the end of the paper. Glue the end in place. Make three more looped shapes and glue together. For the tail, make four more looped shapes again using 40cm (153/4in) lengths of red paper but create longer and therefore fewer loops.

Regal Cardinal Tag

A handsome red cardinal bird sitting upon a silver branch makes a stylish festive tag and provides a good starting point for this theme if you are feeling daunted by the main design. Alternatively, make it to use up any leftover coils and parts that weren't quite right from the main card! The silver branch is glued to a rectangle of green card first and then the bird's body built up from there. All the coils use the same length of paper as for the main card.

Tip . . .

This style of bird could be easily adapted to making a parrot motif by using bright colours, or a fantastical bird using any colours you like.

Finishing the card

Attach all the branches and leaves to the green card before adding the tail and wing to the cardinal bird. Apply a generous amount of glue to the tops of the leaves and along the branches, then sprinkle over ivory Flower Soft® and leave to dry. Shake off the excess Flower Soft® and then attach the tail by just gluing the narrow ends to the bottom of the bird. Mount the bird panel onto cream card and then a dark green card blank. Add a festive greeting if you wish.

Winter Warmer

This red cardinal is caught in a snowstorm, with snowflakes flying all around the bird. By angling the tail feathers horizontally, it creates the impression that the bird is picking its way delicately along the branch, facing the oncoming snow that is dotted all over the card. All the measurements are the same as for the main card, but fewer leaves and branches are needed, so it won't take as much time to complete.

TEMPLATES

SPIRALLING BUTTERFLIES
Page 26

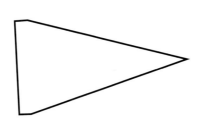

SPLENDID STORK
Page 28

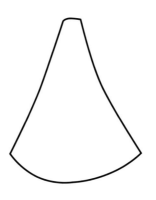

SINGING BLUEBIRDS
Page 30

GRADUATION OWL
Page 48

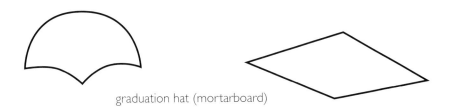

graduation hat (mortarboard)

branch

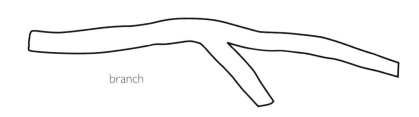

ANT ARMY
Page 22

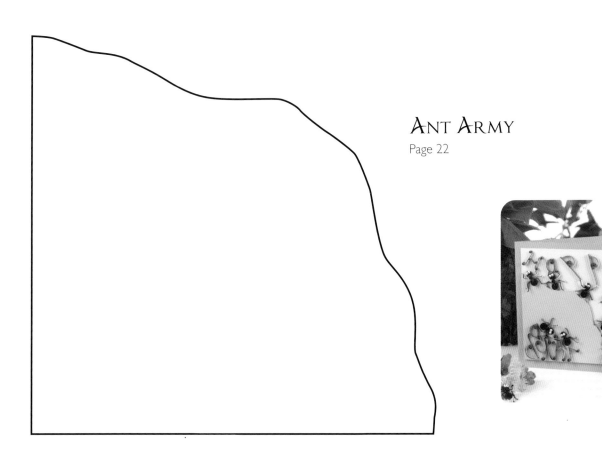

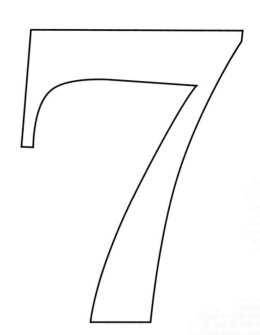

Ladybird Cuties

Page 36

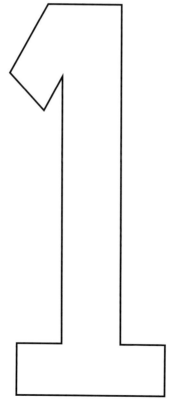
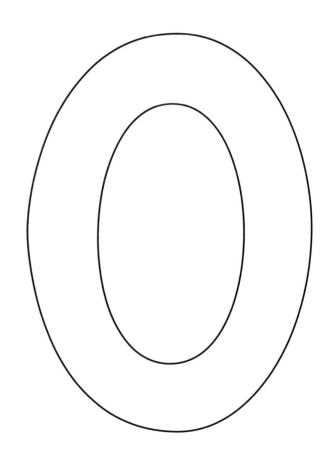

Husking Template and Technique

Page 50–51

The Bejewelled Butterfly on pages 50–51 and variation cards use the technique of husking, where paper strips are wrapped around an arrangement of pins. If you are familiar with this technique, you simply need to copy the template in Step 1 below for the positions of the pins and then refer back to page 50 for the instructions. Beginners to this technique are taken here through the sequence of making the husking shape broken down into two easy steps. The numbers represents the sequence and the black dots where the pins are inserted. Don't insert the pins all at once but one at a time, as illustrated in the photographic steps at the bottom of the page.

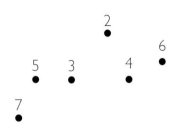

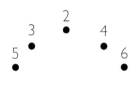

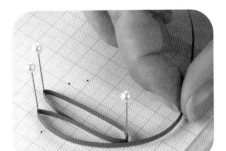
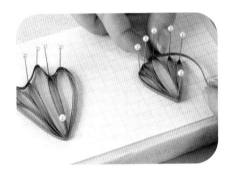

Ant army

Measurements for quilled letters to spell "Happy Birthday" in Ant army pages 22-23 as follows:

H= 5cm (2in), 4cm (1 1/2in), 5cm (2in)
a= 11cm (4 1/2in)
p= 11cm (4 1/2in)
p= 11cm (4 1/2in)
y= 13cm (5in)
B= 5cm, 10cm (4in)
i= 4cm (1 1/2in), 6cm (2 3/8in)

r= 9cm (3 1/2in)
t= 8cm (3 1/8in), 4cm (1 1/2in)
h= 11cm (4 1/2in)
d= 11cm (4 1/2in)
a= 11cm (4 1/2in)
y= 13cm (5in)

SUPPLIERS

UK

Craft Creations
Ingersoll House
Delamare Road
Cheshunt
EN8 9HD
www.craftcreations.com
For peel-off greetings

Elderberry Crafts
17 Elderberry Drive
Dereham
Norfolk
NR20 3ST
www.elderberrycrafts.com

J.J. Quilling Design
29 Hollingworth Road
Petts Wood
Orpington
Kent
BR5 1AQ
www.jjquilling.co.uk

Katy Sue Designs
Henry Robson Way
South Shields
Tyne and Wear
NE33 1RF
www.flower-soft.co.uk

For Flower Soft® products used in
Christmas Cardinal, pages 56–57

Mamelok Papercraft
The Studio
54 Woodfield Lane
Lower Cambourne
Cambridge
CB23 6DS
www.mamelok.com

For decoupage sheets used in
Swooping Seagulls, pages 54–55

USA

Lake City Craft Company
1209 Eaglecrest Street
PO Box 2009
Nixa, Missouri 65714
www.quilling.com

Whimsiquills
25 Indian Run
Enfield
Connecticut 06082-4633
www.whimsiquills.com

AUSTRALIA

Jonathan Mayne
PO Box 345
Mt Martha
VIC 3934
www.jonathanmayne.com.au

USEFUL WEBSITES

Dutch Quilling Guild
www.filigraan.nl

North American Quilling Guild
(NAQG)
www.naqg.org

UK Quilling Guild
www.quilling-guild.co.uk

ABOUT THE AUTHOR

Elizabeth Moad is a busy papercrafter, workshop tutor and author. Elizabeth is accomplished in many crafting techniques but is widely known for her talent in quilling. She is a regular contributor to UK magazines Crafts Beautiful and Let's Make Cards! This is Elizabeth's sixth book and her work has been featured in several other card making books.

Books published by David & Charles, by Elizabeth Moad; *Thrilling Quilling*, *Cards for Lads* and *Dads*, *Quick and Clever Christmas Cards* and *The Papercrafter's Bible*.

ACKNOWLEDGEMENTS

A big "thank you" goes to the team who worked on this project, and made another book possible. Karl Adamson once again provided the professional photography and creative styling. Jo Richardson edited my text with her usual magic to make it enjoyable to read. And thank you to the designers, Sarah Wade (www.designhousestudios.co.uk), Peter Evans and Joanne Steward (www.peterevans-design.co.uk), who worked so speedily and enthusiastically on the layout of this book to create its fabulous look.

INDEX